Robin —

Hope your day begins
with a good Thought!

[signature] 12/2/04

Shortcuts

to
Life's Secrets

Shortcuts
to
Life's Secrets

The Collected Thoughts
of
Hayes McClerkin

Illustrations by Jeffrey Vasquez
Edited by Peggy McClurken

Mountain State Publishing
Martinsburg, West Virginia

Shortcuts to Life's Secrets

Copyright © 2004 by HAYES McCLERKIN

Illustrations Copyright © 2004 by JEFFREY VASQUEZ

Library of Congress Cataloging-in-Publication
Data available upon request

Hardcover ISBN 0-9747005-3-3
Tradepaper ISBN 0-9747005-4-1

LCCN: 2004107840

Published in the United States by
MOUNTAIN STATE PUBLISHING
70 Whitings Neck Road
Martinsburg, West Virginia 25401
304-263-1441
www.mountainstatepublishing.com

First Edition

Cover
Thoughts on Parade
by Jeffrey Vasquez

To Lil,
the mother of our daughters,
Martha, Katherine, and Lauren,
who have given us
eleven wonderful grandchildren,
Carley, Haysen, Zak, Allen, Chrissy,
Olivia, Watson, Dylan, Gaston,
Madison, and Lillian.
They have been the inspiration
for many "thoughts."

Contents

Illustrations

Acknowledgments

Shortcuts to Life's Secrets is a collection of sayings and *thoughts* that are the result of my past and present reading habits, of sermons I've heard, of hymns I've sung, and of good old common sense. In today's world, we all tend to live by sound bites. These *shortcuts* target those of us on the run. The aim is to give a small spoonful of meaning to our busy lives. With the seeds planted, it is my hope that these *thoughts* will be nurtured and they can grow in the minds of the readers and be shared with others.

When I begin to acknowledge and give thanks for all the help in the creation of this work, I find it difficult to know where to begin. The first place, I suppose, is with Luke Sutter, my old navy shipmate. Luke is one of those good friends we rarely find in life but consider ourselves quite lucky when we do.

Had it not been for Luke, I would not have found Peggy McClurken of Mountain State Publishing, whose time, effort, and talents made this book a reality. Peggy has made this project work and in the process found Jeffrey Vasquez, whose illustrations bring many of the *thoughts* to life.

Along the way, many people have encouraged me to publish my *Shortcuts*. They include Connie Berlingeri and Hilary Schaper, wonderful and special friends from Rancho La Puerta in Tecate, Mexico; Jim Gabler, my Beta classmate at Washington and Lee University, and an author in his own right; Sam

Forester, an old friend and business partner; Gary Nutter, a law partner for years and trusted friend.

My trusted legal secretary and assistant for years, Sandy Hartline, has saved and edited my *thoughts* over the years, for which I am grateful. Carolyn Henry, of Arkansas Blue Cross and Blue Shield, who says that I'm at my best when I'm "thinking and driving," has been a steady hand behind the wheel.

Of necessity, I've left out the numerous friends, relatives, and acquaintances who have been the inspiration for many of the thoughts that appear throughout these pages. But, they are all in my heart and in my memories.

Introduction

In 1955, I was serving aboard the USS *Chilton* (APA 38) as a LTJG, a 16-week wonder out of Officer Candidate School. I had never been aboard a ship until I reported to the *Chilton* in December 1953, and less than two years later I found myself as navigator.

Captain C. K. Duncan took command of the ship, and I'm sure he looked at me and must have shuddered at the thought of his naval career being in the hands of a reserve officer from Arkansas. At the time, he didn't know that this was the one and only ship I would serve on in my 43-month navy career. Nor could he have known that he would have a tremendous impact on my life and later successes.

Shortly after he took command, we set sail for Guantanamo Bay, Cuba, for refresher training. Captain Duncan called me into the state room. "Mac," he said, "from this point forward, you are my navigator. I want you to remember this. You are to make the decisions as to what courses we set. Your leadership and the fate of this ship will be determined by the decisions you make. If you have been properly trained, you will make the right decision 95 percent of the time. As to the remaining 5 percent, just admit the error in time to correct it and you will do fine. The main thing is to make a decision. Indecision causes failure. All officers, including those on watch, will shortly be in a meeting with me in the ward room. You will be the only officer on watch. Go now and relieve the officer of the deck."

That short talk has remained with me all my life. Captain Duncan retired as a full admiral. I did not ruin his career. My father died when I was 10 years old, and looking back on my life, I now see that Captain Duncan was the first male figure to put his trust in me for something the consequences of which could have a significant impact on his life and the lives of many. The brevity of his speech in no way condensed the meaning.

Too often, we get lost in our words and say nothing. *Shortcuts to Life's Secrets* was first conceived as short messages to my daughters. Being normal children, I knew they would likely not listen to or read anything of great length. The memory of Captain Duncan came back, as did his communications style: *Say in as few words as necessary what needs to be said to get the point across.*

Thus, with brevity, but in words that could be clearly understood, I e-mailed my first "Thought for the Day:" *It is hard to kick a moving ass.* Subsequent *thoughts* dealt with human relations, with human weaknesses, with who we are as individuals, and with the importance of meaning in our lives. They can best be summed up with: *Life is like a yo-yo, with lots of ups and down. The important thing is not to let the string break.*

Hopefully, the following pages, with thoughts illustrations, and author's commentaries, will give you some inspiration in facing the day-to-day grind that the 21st Century dictates. This book is intended to be food for thought.

Enjoy and share.

Success

"Everyone aims high
but not all have the nerve
to pull the trigger."

Can You Pull the Trigger?

Risk-taking is the key to success. Someone once pointed out that when the apple is at the end of the limb, the best way to get it is to climb right out on the limb and pick it. If you try to get it by hugging the trunk of the tree, you'll end up with nothing but bark burns and wonder why you never succeeded. The limb may break and you may fall, but successful people climb right back up the tree and try again.

I have told my children that we are born with about six bullets with which to hit success in our belt of life. You must have the guts, though, to pull the trigger. You may miss or you may hit something you didn't expect, but don't go to your grave with bullets left in your belt. Many people can't pull the trigger out of fear, and as they near the end of a modest career, they wonder why they didn't go further up the ladder of success. Many waste their bullets on trivia or on wanting what someone else has, but they at least pulled the trigger and took a chance.

I once read about advice Warren Buffett gave to a young man. He told the fellow to imagine himself at home plate, waiting for a pitch. When a good pitch is thrown, he said, you must "swing from the heels." The successful Buffett proffered that far too few people have the courage to do that and go through life opting instead to safely bunt.

Thoughts for Success

*Success is measured not so much by
the position one has reached but by the
obstacles one has overcome in getting there.*

*Opportunity is missed by many people because
it is dressed in overalls and looks like work.*

*You are not a failure if you fall down,
but you are if you don't get back up.*

*Never allow what you cannot do
interfere with what you can do.*

*There are those who do the work and
those who take the credit. Try to be in the
first group because there's less competition.*

*If you are going to have a successful tomorrow,
you better have a positive today.*

3

*Success isn't shaped by what happens
to you; it is the result of what you do
with what happens to you.*

Failure is success as long as you learn from it.

There is no past tense for the word opportunity.

*Successful people are not afraid
to go against the crowd.*

The secret of getting ahead is getting started.

*The most rewarding way to get to the top
is by lifting those beneath you.*

*It is easy to give up, but when you do,
that is as far as you will go.*

Successful people don't waste time
trying to be like someone else.

Failure is temporary; success is permanent.

True success, like true happiness,
is not spelled with dollar signs.

> **When opportunity knocks,
> make sure you are not
> in the backyard looking
> for a four-leaf clover.**

If you never take a risk, you will miss the
valuable lesson of learning from your mistakes.

At the end of each day make sure
your good deeds are in the majority.
That is the democratic way to success.

5

*Everybody dreams of success but few
take the time to figure out what it means.*

*If all you do is think about the times you failed,
you won't have time to succeed.*

*Define success for yourself;
don't accept someone else's definition for it.*

*It is hard to be a winner if you don't
have a goal line to cross.*

*The shortest path to success
is not necessarily the surest.*

*Risk can result in reward or failure.
Doing nothing will result in nothing.*

*The biggest obstacle on your road to success
is an inflated ego.*

*You have to get through today before
you can have a successful tomorrow.*

*To be a winner you must accept mistakes
as part of success.*

*Dreamers rarely succeed until
they wake up to reality.*

*People who think they know everything
often get an education in failure.*

*Make sure your values are higher
than your ambitions.*

*It is hard to find success when you
judge it by what others have done.*

*Success is defined, not by how far you go,
but by the steps you take in the right direction.*

A full life is determined as much by the number of failures you have surmounted as the number of successes you have achieved.

Following the crowd will only get you where everyone else is going.

Success comes when you understand how to turn an idea into reality.

Remember that the people you use as steps on the way up won't be there on the way down.

A good way to get ahead in life is to put other people first.

If you depend on someone else to be your motivation, you will go only as far as they go.

*Bull baffles brains 90 percent of the time
but will only get you 10 percent of the way
up the ladder of success.*

*Most people fail on the fast road to success
because they can't take the sharp curves.*

Indecision is a key to failure, not success.

*The best way to reach the top is to start at the
bottom. Then you know how far it is to fall.*

*If you get to the top by climbing
on others' backs, make sure they
don't leave you hanging.*

*Success is measured by the number
of people you help along the way,
not how many you step on to get there.*

**Success is defined by the number
of failures we survive.**

*The best way to avoid shooting yourself
in the foot in life is to aim high.*

*To really be successful is to always
remember those who got you started.*

*People don't necessarily miss opportunities;
often, they are afraid to take them.*

*Failure means you tried;
success means you overcame failure.*

*How you define success depends a lot
on how you feel about yourself.*

*The road to success is littered with people who
think change is about putting on
clean underwear.*

*Success is determined by how you
maneuver the curves in the road of life.*

Fear and risk are two different words;
fear of risk is defined as failure.

The biggest obstacle to your success
might be between your ears.

There is no road map to success or happiness;
you have to blaze our own trail.

> ***A key to getting ahead***
> ***in life is to pull people up,***
> ***not put them down.***

True success is not measured in dollars but in
how you handle the ups and downs of life and
what you contribute along the way.

Success is a moving target,
so sitting on your laurels won't find it.

*One huge stumbling block to success
is a big ego.*

Successful people ask how, not why.

*Life is not a straight road; success is
determined by how well you take the curves.*

*Success today depends largely on how well
you forget the failures of yesterday.*

*Look at risk as a key to success,
not an unknown enemy to be feared.*

*In the race of life, the people who don't
succeed have often stumbled over themselves.*

Fear of failure is not the key to success.

*It is difficult to be successful
if you are afraid to set goals.*

*A person who climbs to the top on the
backs of others has a very shaky foundation.*

*Inspiration is not complete until
you mix it with perspiration.*

*"I have told my children that we
are born with about six bullets with
which to hit success in our belt of
life. You must have the guts though
to pull the trigger. You may miss or
you may hit something you didn't
expect, but don't go to your grave
with bullets left in your belt."*

*Success in life is determined by
how you handle mistakes.*

*The strong and successful always have
a diet of moral fiber.*

*Successful people don't fear change,
they challenge it.*

*Success in life is not based on how smart you
are but on how you use the smarts you have.*

*Never let success shorten your memory
of those who got you there.*

*Successful people never run out of time.
Time runs out on them.*

*Successful people control anger.
Anger controls unsuccessful people.*

*When you turn dreams into goals,
success follows.*

*Success will never come if you are waiting
on someone else to find it for you.*

15

*Success in your life depends upon
how you handle envy and greed.*

*Success is hard to find if you keep looking
in the same places.*

*Life is a series of ups and downs, and
a key to success is getting up from the downs.*

*Success is a steep hill to climb, which is why
many people give up before they reach the top.*

*Success is measured not only by what you
have, but also by what you leave behind.*

*Two keys to success—a warm smile and
kind words—are free but not so freely given.*

*Success and happiness depend on
how you tolerate the pain of change.*

> # *If you let success go to your head, your backside will begin to show.*

We all have baggage in our lives. The successful learn to carry it better than others.

Successful people recognize the cost of wasted time.

Successful people see failure as another opportunity to succeed.

The unknown is a challenge, not a fear, to the successful person.

Resting on your laurels can wear a hole in your success.

*Failure is often a result of
not finishing what you started.*

*How far you will go for others will have a great
impact on how far you will go in life yourself.*

*Satisfy yourself that you have properly defined
success before you say you have achieved it.*

*Success depends on having the foresight to not
let today's decision be tomorrow's mistake.*

*Learn the difference between self-confidence
and ego and you have made a great stride
on the road to success.*

*Success achived at the expense of others
is fool's gold.*

Fear of failure causes waste of talent.

**How soon the door to success opens
depends on how hard we are
willing to knock.**

*If you don't improve on today's success,
you are looking at tomorrow's failure.*

*A key to success and happiness
is to love others more than yourself.*

*Success depends on how you control yourself,
not how you control other people.*

*Mistakes are part of life. What you do with
your mistakes determines success or failure.*

*Successful people let their actions
rather than their mouths speak for them.*

*Change is a challenge; success depends on
one's willingness to accept the challenge.*

*The steps in your ladder to success
are often failures you have overcome.*

> ## *A key to success is turning imagination into reality.*

*A successful person understands
that mixing greed and arrogance
produces only illegitimate offspring.*

*Successful people concentrate on what
they know, not what someone else knows.*

*Failure is a temporary event;
only you can make it linger.*

*Successful people define their surroundings;
others let their surroundings define them.*

*A person afraid to take risks always wonders
why others have what she wants.*

*Fear of failure will cause you to
miss the challenges of life and leave you
wondering why your life is so dull.*

*A successful person knows that to get ahead
in life there are times when it is wise
to let others finish first.*

*There is a fine line between success and failure.
Fortunately we all have the opportunity
to draw that line.*

**The successful leader uses the
word "include;" the arrogant
leader only knows "exclude."**

*Successful people never allow time
to be a wasted asset.*

*If you take shortcuts on the road of life,
you could end up with detours
on the road to success.*

*The successful person works on
correcting mistakes rather than
gloating over achievements.*

*It is diffficult to succeed by wondering why.
The real key is asking how.*

*It is hard to come in first
if all you seek is to make the team.*

*Success may be just around the corner. The
challenge is having the nerve to turn the corner.*

*If your idea of success is based on envy,
you will always be at the end of the line.*

*It is easy to follow others; the challenge in life
comes when you get to the head of the line.*

One's mind is the key to success.
Unfortunately, many of us misplace the key.

If you spell $ucce$$ with dollar signs,
you take the meaning out of life.

Your success depends not on what you know,
but on knowing what you need to know.

Success comes to those who have lofty ideas
but still keep their feet on the ground.

True success comes when you are able
to align your dreams with reality.

If you let success go to your head,
you will be a failure to those around you.

"Our" way will always result in
greater success than "my" way.

You have to stick your neck out
to get ahead, but always be careful
not to put it on a chopping block.

Take care to never let anticipation of success
get in the way of planning for success.

A vital key to success is knowing
when it is better to finish second.

Never forget that you may find success
at the end of a string of failures.

It is when you think you are indispensable
that others begin to think you are dispensable.

Successful people substitute
planning for worry.

*It is difficult to see high hopes succeed
when they are propelled by hot air.*

*Success in life means getting back up
from getting knocked down.*

*Some people blast their way to the top;
others climb the ladder. It's amazing
how fast the former can fall.*

*Success in life is measured not only
by how high you have risen, but also by
the number of people you brought with you.*

Prejudice

ℭ

*"A narrow-minded person
has tunnel vision and misses
a lot of beautiful scenery
along the road of life."*

Understanding Prejudice

As a young child growing up in Arkansas during the 1930s and '40s, I remember segregation as a way of life. Yet, other than being segregated, I didn't know *prejudice,* as it was called. Prejudice is an attitude one has to learn.

My grandmother, Virginia Rogers Maloney, had a father and a father-in-law who both went off to fight for the Confederacy. But, there was not a prejudicial bone in her body when it came to race. Politics was another matter. She quit talking to her neighbor across the street because he didn't vote for Roosevelt.

Grandmother was affectionately known around Monticello, Arkansas, as *Miss Jenny.* She drove a grey Ford A model coupe. When she decided it was too much effort on her part to drive—mainly because her car quit—she moved from the *old place* outside of town into her *town place.* The former was a pre-Civil War house with large oak trees in the front and a functioning well between the kitchen and main house. The latter was not in use because Miss Jenny had "running water."

Behind the town place was a garden and *rent house.* A black man named Major—who to a child looked to be as old as dirt—lived in the rent house. He paid no rent, and my grandmother was proud of the fact that he had indoor plumbing. She always said, "We have to tend to Major because the Germans gassed him during the war." I never knew him by any name but Major, nor did I know how he got the name or if he was really gassed by the Germans. I didn't care because he was the wisest man I knew and he could whistle in spite of being gassed and whittle.

When I visited my grandmother, I looked forward to her mince meat pie and Major. He entranced me with stories and we would spend hours lying in the back yard looking for four-leaf clovers. He would say, "four-leaf clovers brings you luck 'cause they pointin' in all four directions." I wish he could have met my wife because I can picture him saying, "Missa Hayes, yo sho' did marry up."

As a teenager, I went for a visit, and Major was gone. I lost a friend.

My home in Texarkana was not much different. My mother was what one might call a benevolent segregationist. *Separate-but-equal* ideas were practiced, but racial slurs were not allowed in the house.

With my separate-but-equal background, I went off to college and the navy, never giving much thought to the indignity of racial separation. On the USS *Chilton,* we had a chief stewards mate, a handsome black man who had served with distinction in World War II. His home was Philadelphia, and once a shipmate and I happened to be driving there for a wedding. The chief asked if he could catch a ride. We agreed because he was a good man and a shipmate.

My friend was driving, and being from Long Island knew nothing of segregation. He wanted to stop along the way on the eastern shore of Maryland, but I knew that the chief would not be allowed to eat with us. When we reached Delaware, I thought the climate would be more friendly and suggested we stop at a roadside cafe. The three of us went in—the chief in his uniform with all his battle ribbons—and sat down.

The waitress came over and said, "We don't serve *n------* in here." I immediately saw the hurt in the chief's eyes. We got up to leave, and I said in as slow a southern drawl as I could muster, "I'm from Arkansas, and if he is good enough to eat with me, we are all too good to eat in this damn joint."

The chief could never look me in the eye again. In his mind, the waitress had destroyed him as a man in my eyes, and I could feel the hurt. That day, I knew the pain of prejudice.

Thoughts on Prejudice

Attitude can have a great influence on how you look upon and treat those who are different.

CB

If all you do is prejudge people, it doesn't leave time to love them.

CB

If you only see what you want to see in people, you miss a lot of beautiful sights.

CB

It would be a better world if we looked up to more people than we look down on.

CB

If God wanted us all to be alike, we would all have the same thumb print.

CB

First impressions can be misleading; remember we eat eggs in spite of the smell coming from the henhouse.

*Judge yourself by the same standards
you set for others.*

ᘓ

*You will never see much if you keep
looking down your nose at others.*

ᘓ

*What we think of other people depends
a great deal on how we think of ourselves.*

ᘓ

*Many people try to mask their insecurity
in life with prejudice.*

ᘓ

*If you look down on people for
being different, don't expect others
to look up to you.*

ᘓ

*There is no cost for loving others,
but the cost of prejudice is high.*

ᘓ

*A person who looks down on others
doesn't stand very tall in the eyes of tolerance.*

ભ

*Admire those who rise from humble beginnings,
but be wary of those who forget
from where they came.*

ભ

*A narrow-minded person has a difficult time
expanding his circle of friends.*

ભ

*If you look for the good in someone you will
find good; if you look for the bad you will
find bad. So, always look for the good.*

ભ

*It is better to have varying degrees of love
for everyone than no love at all.*

ભ

*Make sure you live by the same rules
by which you prejudge others.*

ભ

*A person who looks down on others
often has an over-inflated ego.*

಴

*If you have to look down on someone
to feel good about yourself, you put yourself
at the bottom of the pecking order.*

಴

*You have real heart trouble when you are
prejudiced against people you don't know.*

಴

*It is easy to hate those who are different
because we are lazy with our love.*

಴

*When confronting prejudice, the meaning and
significance of Easter can't be topped.*

಴

*It takes more effort to love than hate,
but the dividends are much greater.*

಴

*Remember, you are judged by
how you treat other people.*

಴

Compassion is easy to say but hard to express.

34

ೞ

*Judgmental people generally get judged
by their own judgments.*

ೞ

The only way to open a closed
mind is with an open heart.

ೞ

*You will be better person if you look at others
with love rather than prejudice or hate.*

ೞ

Judgment is easy to pass but hard to receive.

ೞ

*Before you pass judgment on another,
walk in that person's shoes to see if they fit.*

ೞ

*Tolerance and compassion for your fellow man
will put real meaning in your life.*

ೞ

*When you look down on someone, you
expose your backside for them to look up to.*

✃

*It is easy to judge others because
that helps us overlook our own faults.*

✃

*When you look down your nose at someone,
all you are smelling is yourself.*

✃

*A prejudicial person spends half her life
looking down on other people,
then wonders where all her time went.*

✃

*How you judge other people will determine
how other people judge you.*

✃

Look in the mirror before you judge others.

✃

*It is the wise man who looks in the mirror
. before he prejudges others.*

✃

Prejudice is a self-inflicted wound.

*Hate is contagious,
and must be treated with
strong doses of kindness.*

☙

Open minds create love;
closed minds spawn hate.

☙

Narrow-minded people miss many of the joys
of life because they can't see the big picture.

☙

Prejudice will destroy your soul.

☙

It is easy to hate a bigot, but don't let
that hate take you to the same level.

☙

It is easy to spot discrimination but hard to
accept that you may be part of the problem.

☙

Hate can cause heart trouble.

℃ℬ

*Lack of understanding is
the breeding ground for hate.*

℃ℬ

*Show the same respect for those below you
as you do for those above you.*

℃ℬ

*If you have to judge a person, judge by what
they do rather than by who they are.*

℃ℬ

> *"The waitress came over and
> said, 'We don't serve n------ in
> here.' I immediately saw the hurt
> in the chief's eyes....In his mind,
> the waitress had destroyed him
> as a man in my eyes, and I could
> feel the hurt. That day, I knew
> the pain of prejudice."*

℃ℬ

Lack of tolerance is a sure sign of insecurity.

39

೫

*Prejudice is the greatest obstacle
to understanding.*

೫

*If you think someone is different from you,
remember they may be thinking
the same thing about you.*

೫

*It is hard to be loving and judgmental
at the same time.*

೫

*Hate dies with you; love lives forever
like the fountain of youth.*

೫

*Prejudice and hate will make your life seem
like a ping pong ball, empty and small.*

೫

The end result of a closed mind is a fool.

೫

*Bad breath and prejudice have one thing
in common, both offend people.*

ℭℬ

*Prejudice is the illness of a small mind
that won't take its medicine, namely love.*

ℭℬ

*Pride can be a wonderful trait unless
you turn it into prejudice.*

ℭℬ

**Hate and prejudice spawn
the same result, leaving bigots
in the cess pool of life.**

ℭℬ

*A person who looks down his nose at others
has a problem seeing the big picture of life.*

ℭℬ

*Hate and prejudice will give you heart trouble;
the only cure is love.*

ℭℬ

*The prejudicial person is insecure; the loving
person is secure. The choice is yours.*

Never try to mask prejudice or intolerance with patriotism.

⌘

It is a difficult job to hate,
but we spend a lot of time doing it.

⌘

A narrow-minded person has tunnel vision
and misses a lot of beautiful scenery
along the road of life.

⌘

Narrow minds usually cause
wide differences between people.

⌘

It is a sign of strength, not weakness, to admit
your insecurities and prejudices. If you don't,
you will have a heavy burden to carry.

⌘

People who look down on their fellow man
should look at their own shortcomings
before passing judgment.

⌘

Bigot is another word for
a little person.

Time

*"If you define age as a state of mind,
rather than a number of years,
you have discovered the
fountain of youth."*

Does Age Really Count?

We all worry about aging, but unfortunately we can't stop the clock from ticking. Nor should we want to. When the clock stops ticking for each of us, we no longer have to worry about aging.

A friend of mine, who is a couple years older than I, remarked about my age, "You are about to catch up with me."

"You better hope I don't catch up with you," I replied.

"Why?" he asked.

"Because," I said, "When I do, it means you have stopped."

As I approached the occasion of my 50th high school reunion, I was brought back to memories of my graduation. The first class to graduate from our high school was in 1899, and the class had one male. At my graduation ceremony in 1949, commemorating the 50th anniversary of the school, that man gave the commencement address. I vividly remember thinking he must be the oldest person I had ever seen, and surely he would require help getting off the stage. Some 50 years later, I now find myself in his shoes and am proud to say I neither need nor want assistance getting off the stage.

A 77-year-old friend of mine commented that he thinks of someone as being old if that person is 10 years older than he. And, of course that 10-year span is a continually moving target.

I have found that age, like many other aspects of life, has a lot to do with what is between one's ears. We have all known people who cannot tolerate change. These individuals tend to age rapidly simply because they act old. At the opposite extreme are people who seem to stay 17-years-young in thoughts and actions. Then, there are those who enjoy the advantages of advanced age but still think young.

At a recent cocktail party, a friend of mine pointed out a woman standing nearby who had undergone several face lifts. "All she did was end up looking like Phyllis Diller," my friend said.

Another friend commented on the one thing bothering him about getting older. "I don't mind the young girls saying 'no,'" he said. "It's when they say 'no, sir' that hurts."

Thoughts About Time

The bad thing about good things is they come to an end; the good thing about bad things is with time they too come to an end.

Tomorrow has a difficult time coming if you keep worrying about yesterday.

Tomorrow's friend may be today's enemy.

Don't be afraid to confront your past; the only time it will hurt you is when you relive it.

If you spend today worrying about yesterday, you will never have a tomorrow.

If you set goals and pursue them, you will forget all about your age.

Today may not be forever, but it is all we have.

*If you spend your time worrying
about tomorrow's perceived problems,
you will miss today's pleasures.*

*Tomorrow's sunrise will be brighter if you let
today's sunset wipe your slate clean.*

*If you keep worrying about the hereafter,
you will lose the here-and-now.*

*Many people think yesterday
will get them through today,
and they end up with no tomorrow.*

*How you end each day has a bearing
on how you begin each tomorrow.*

*If you are afraid of change,
don't look in the mirror.*

*A sure way for the past to catch up with you
is to keep looking back.*

> ## *Yesterday is history. Tomorrow is a dream. Today is reality.*

*You won't go very far if you keep waiting
for the right time to do something.*

*Don't worry about time passing;
if it didn't we would not be here.*

*Time never shows up on the balance sheet
until it is wasted.*

*Don't worry about your age.
What matters is the miles you've traveled
and the roads you've chosen.*

*It is better to waste money than time.
You can make more money,
but time lost can never be recovered.*

Time is a gift; use it wisely.

*If you set goals and pursue them,
you will forget your age.*

*A sure way to ruin today is to have guilt about
yesterday and anxiety about tomorrow.*

*As you grow older, you learn
the only thing you can control is yourself.*

*Don't overlook the pleasures of today by
looking forward to the promises of tomorrow.*

*Time never stands still, but if you do,
it will leave you behind.*

*The best way to have a good ending is to
start with a good beginning.*

*When you have time on your hands,
you are losing the feel for your future.*

A bad day is 24 hours long, just like the rest;
only you can make it longer.

The more you worry about old age,
the older you get.

If you live in the past,
yesterday was your future.

A person who runs from the present
will never have a future.

People who have to buy future respect
for themselves are likely trying to cover up
their not-so-noble pasts.

Most people don't place a value on time
until they are left wondering where it has gone.

Time is like money;
you don't appreciate it until it runs out.

*Age doesn't mean growing old
until you plant that thought there.*

*If you look at life as today and not tomorrow,
old age will never arrive.*

Live for today, and let old age come later.

*The key to cultivating good memories
for tomorrow is doing good deeds today.*

*We seem to waste a lot of time
trying to be what we can't be.*

*Dreaming about tomorrow or worrying
about yesterday will only make you
miss out on the realities of today.*

*The best way for the past to catch up
with you is to keep looking back.*

If your day starts off bad, lighten up.
Keep reminding yourself that it is
just another crappy day in paradise.

Yesterday is only a block on the calendar.
To have a good today, let it stay there.

A sure way to grow old fast is to
keep company with unhappy people.

Slow people age fast.

If all your days were the same, you would have
no past memories and no future dreams.

A young mind will carry an old
body along with it.

If you can be proud of what you do today,
it is easy to build a foundation for tomorrow.

Don't worry about time. You can't stop it.

*The more you live in the past,
the more you realize your age.*

*The person who keeps busy
does not have time to grow old.*

*Today is all we have, but always remember,
the same will be said about tomorrow.*

*Memories are of the past, but
without them there would be no future.*

*If all you yearn for is the "good old days"
of yesterday, you will miss the
great new todays and tomorrows.*

*Memories can be wonderful on rainy days;
just don't let them cloud your future dreams.*

The best way to grow old fast
is to stop growing your brain.

You can waste time and regret it,
or you can cherish time and be fulfilled.

The best way to spoil a perfectly good today
is by trying to relive yesterday.

A person who wants tomorrow to be like
yesterday generally is having a bad today.

A sure way to grow old fast is to
worry about growing old.

How you find today may have a great deal
to do with how you left yesterday.

Growing old is an individual process,
determined by how a person defines 'old.'

The fountain of youth is your mind; aging
does not have to be perceived as growing old.

Good health and prosperity help us
paint over the rust that surrounds us.

*Don't be so proud of your past that
it could make you ashamed of today.*

**"A friend of mine said of getting
old, 'I don't mind the young girls
saying no. It's when they say
no, sir that hurts.'"**

*If you don't think things have changed,
don't throw away last year's calendar.*

*Never let the fear of tomorrow
spoil the fun of today.*

*Don't let yesterday's regrets
become today's problems.*

*Time doesn't seem quite so important
until it has run out.*

TIME

*Time never stands still and all too often
leaves us wondering where it went.*

*If you define age as a state of mind,
rather than a number of years,
you have discovered the fountain of youth.*

*When the racehorse of time stands still,
you have answered the final bugle call.*

*How you waste your time is your business;
just make sure it doesn't show up
on your boss's ledger sheet.*

*Time is never wasted
when it is spent loving others.*

*Since time never stands still, we have to keep
changing to keep up with the times.*

*The beauty of youth is that the
"good old days" don't get in the way.*

59

The sands of time are gone forever as they pass through the hourglass, but on the body, they merely shift from place to place.

Never forget that tomorrow, today will have become part of the "good old days."

Remember the past, but don't let it ruin the present.

People looking for the "good old days" have a difficult time understanding they are all in the cemetery.

People who drag the past around are running the race of life with their shoelaces tied together.

Wasted time leaves no memories.

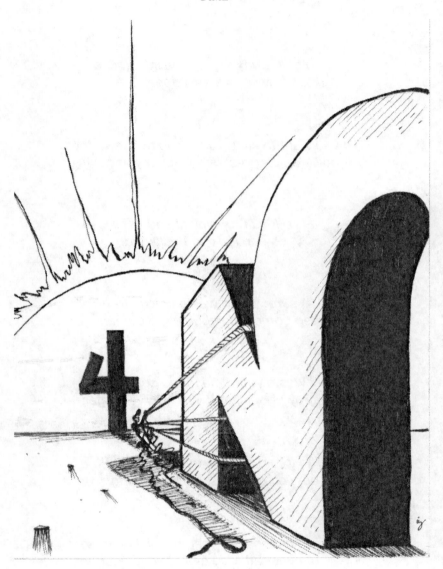

**It is a heavy load to get through today
if you are still hauling yesterday around.**

*Don't let today's doing be influenced
by yesterday's done.*

*If you want to keep your head above water
today, don't let yesterday weigh you down.*

*It is difficult to think ahead when
you keep looking backward.*

*A sure way to waste time is to
keep comparing yourself to others.*

*Don't waste your time in the company of
unhappy people, and you will live longer.*

*The future may be hard to predict,
but you can be sure it is coming.*

*You can't change the year in which you were
born, but your attitude can change your age.*

**Time can't be recycled,
so be careful not to waste it.**

*Dragging the past around is like
traveling the road of life on flat tires.*

*Solving today's problems will make
tomorrow's memories brighter.*

*In aging, never forget that positive attitudes
live longer than negative thoughts.*

*Never forget that your future is yesterday
if you live in the past.*

*Unbagging the past or getting wrapped up
in the future keeps us from
opening the gift of today.*

*When you reject anger as a waste of time,
your days will happier and you will be healthier.*

If time is valuable, why waste it?

*Time will tell how old you are,
but attitude will determine your age.*

*Happiness has a changing definition with the
passage of time; just don't let your clock stop.*

**A fool wishes to be young again;
the wise man seeks to get
the most out of what time is left.**

*Ironically, many people who yearn for
the "good old days" are reluctant to leave
their air-conditioned houses.*

Ego

*"Never permit your ego to get so big
that you can't pass through
the window of opportunity
when it opens."*

Spelling Ego With a Little "e"

In 1969, I was elected Speaker of the House of Representatives of the state of Arkansas. At the time, I was the youngest speaker in the history of the state at age 37. The governor was of a different party—unusual at the time—and upon my shoulders fell the responsibility to lead the way for our party. The speaker controlled the budgets of the state and therefore wielded a great deal of power—or at least he thought he did.

As time went by, my ego began to get larger and larger, not unusual for a politician. I thought I could be governor, and a few people around me thought the same. They were under the influence of my ego. Ten people began to sound like 10,000. Off I ran. Part of our campaign strategy was to flood the state with billboards that would make my name a household word.

One day, while campaigning in north Arkansas, we stopped to gas up the campaign car. While the driver was filling the tank, I spied a woman filling her tank and went over to her. I handed her a campaign card and said, "Hi, my name is Hayes McClerkin and I'm running for governor." To this she replied, "What state?" I realized then that the billboards were not working.

I lost the primary. It taught me to spell ego with a little e, little g, and little o. I learned that an out-of-control ego can lead one down many a wrong path in life, a fact I later used to my advantage.

After politics, I resumed an active practice of law in the energy field. This took me to places like Los Angeles, Houston, New Orleans, Denver, Dallas, and other large cities where I dealt with "high rise" lawyers. These are lawyers who practice on the 26th floor of a large office building and think they are smarter than everyone else because they can look down on them.

When dealing with these types, I would look around in amazement and be impressed by the altitude, then talk in the slowest Arkansas nasal drawl I could muster. I could see the other lawyers swell up and begin to think, "this is the most ignorant son of a bitch I've ever seen." It only worked for a little while, but long enough for that "high rise" lawyer's ego to get in the way.

Thoughts on Ego

*Half the people on earth have something to say
and don't say it; the other half have
nothing to say but keep saying it.*

*If you can't play hurt, you probably
won't make the first team.*

*A person's ego is his worst enemy because
it often gets in the way of opportunity.*

*The most important word in a person's
vocabulary is "we" and the least important is "I."*

*When you talk, don't say something
to make you look good; say it to make
the other person feel good.*

*The best way to lose your self-confidence
is to feel sorry for yourself.*

EGO

*Make sure you laugh at yourself before
you laugh at someone else.*

*The best way to start losing friends is to tell
everybody how sorry you feel for yourself.*

*People who brag about themselves to others
usually don't have much to look at in the mirror.*

Many so-called experts are self-anointed.

Self-pity is akin to wearing wet socks.

Ego is a small word that causes big problems.

*If you can't poke fun at yourself,
don't laugh at someone else.*

Little people often hide behind big egos.

*A person who enjoys power
will eventually be overpowered.*

A big ego is never as effective as a little humility.

Always thinking you are right never leaves open the possibility you are wrong.

A self-centered person travels in a small and ever-decreasing circle.

Humility never wears thin to those around you.

The best way to lose your self-confidence is to feel sorry for yourself.

A two-legged jackass is born of a big ego.

The more you think of yourself, the less others will think of you.

EGO

*People who get wrapped up in themselves
don't realize that others laugh
at their packaging.*

*Ninety-eight percent of the people don't care
about your problems, and the other
two percent already know about them.*

*If you can't laugh at yourself, you may be
missing what everyone else finds so funny.*

*A sure way to waste time
is to think only of yourself.*

Big egos usually are born of little minds.

*A self-centered person is a
very small package under the tree of life.*

*Until you accept yourself,
you will have a difficult time
getting others to take you seriously.*

*You will always find that a lot of
empty space surrounds big egos.*

*Self-centered people are generally unhappy
because they have no outside interests.*

*If all you can talk about is your problems,
you will soon be talking to yourself.*

*A self-centered person will have
a very small circle of friends.*

*A sure way to be a big person is
to take time for the little people.*

**A big ego never allows you
to look down to see who
you are stepping on.**

Self-centered people will implode from envy.

72

*It is difficult to understand others
if you don't know who you are.*

*Small egos don't get in the way of solving
big problems, but big egos can make
solving small problems difficult.*

*Every once in a while you should listen to your
self because that is what other people hear.*

*If you depend on material possessions
and good looks to feel good,
you are leading a shallow life.*

*One who lives only for herself
is living with a bore.*

*If you can't enjoy yourself, don't be surprised
that other people find you a bore.*

*People who think more of themselves than they
do of others have only their egos as friends.*

*People who feel sorry for themselves
run the race of life in worn out sneakers.*

*It is difficult to make friends
when the person you admire the most
is the face you see in the mirror.*

Great minds can be made small by big egos.

*Most people are blind to their own egos
but readily recognize them in others.*

*A big ego is like an untied shoe;
both can make you trip and fall.*

*If all you do is try to please the person in the
mirror, you need to have your values checked.*

*When you feel sorry for yourself,
you drink from the toilet of life.*

*People who think only of themselves
have very little on their minds.*

*Before we can be all things for others,
we have to figure out who we are ourselves.*

> ### *Feeling sorry for yourself is about as helpful as taking a shower with your clothes on.*

*If you are going to feel sorry for yourself,
keep it a secret.*

*Feeding an ego will never add weight
or substance to what others think of you.*

*In our efforts to puff ourselves up, we overlook
that we are not impressing those around us.*

*A self-proclaimed expert is the product
of an over-blown ego.*

*If you can't find fault in yourself, you will
never solve the problems bothering you.*

*If you worship what other people think of you,
your heart is in the wrong place.*

*It is difficult to like someone else
if you are not comfortable with yourself.*

*If you live only for yourself,
you will miss the joy of sharing with others.*

*Self-centered people traveling the road of life
see only what is in their rear view mirror.*

*It is difficult to see the real world
if you can't look beyond yourself.*

*Pride and ego will blind you to reality
and lead you down the dark path to failure.*

**Self-pity is the dog,
and your life is the fireplug.**

> ## *The shame of life is that we feel sorry for ourselves more than we show concern for others.*

*If you get wrapped up in yourself,
you may be the only present under the tree.*

*The good in a person goes unnoticed
when he becomes self-centered.*

*A self-centered person might go a lot further
if he didn't have to haul around a big ego.*

*Good minds are wasted
when consumed by self-pity.*

*Pride is a great attribute until
it gets in the way of common sense.*

*Self-centered people are very nearsighted
and miss a lot of the beauty around them.*

If we showed concern for others
as much as we worry about ourselves,
think what a better world this would be.

How you see the world depends a great deal
on the perspective you have of yourself.

If you want to ruin your day,
start it off by feeling sorry for yourself.

If humility looks so good
on others, why don't we try
more of it on ourselves?

There is a fine line between pride and ego.
Unfortunately, when you cross over,
others will recognize it before you do.

Isn't it amazing how success has a way
of inflating one's ego?

*If we spent as much time and money
making our thoughts as beautiful as our faces,
the world would be a more attractive place.*

*Pride and ego will always
cloud prudent judgment.*

A big fat ego exposes a small narrow mind.

*Common sense and a big ego
make unlikely roommates.*

*A politician has a major problem when
he lets his ego outrun his popularity.*

Out-of-control egos generally outrun talent.

The best cure for a big ego is a little humility.

*Many of the problems in our lives
are the product of our egos.*

> # On the road of life, your ego is like an automobile; the smaller it is, the more mileage you get.

A little humility will go a long way, but it will always have trouble getting around a big ego.

It is difficult to hide behind big egos because they are transparent.

A self-centered person has a difficult time seeing the big picture of life.

The best way to build a healthy ego is to feel good about yourself by helping others.

If carrying a big ego around doesn't tire you, it certainly wears on those around you.

*An out-of-control ego must be housebroken
like a new puppy or all you will do
is clean up after it.*

*A person who is wrapped up in himself
lives in a very small box.*

Big egos live in fear of running into bigger egos.

*A big ego often comes across to others
as the rear end of an elephant.*

If you want a boring life, think only of yourself.

*Self-centered people and bad breath have a lot
in common; others want to avoid both.*

A big ego can make a jackass walk on two legs.

*Ego is only a three letter word,
but it can cause four-letter problems.*

EGO

Pride comes from what you have done;
ego comes from what you think you have done.

The more you think of yourself,
the more you paint yourself in a corner.

The best friend a self-centered person
will ever have is her mirror.

Never forget that other people don't see
the same person you see in the mirror.

When we get wrapped up in ourselves,
we become such a small package
no one wants to see what's inside.

Love has a way of becoming self-centered
unless you share it.

Altruism has a difficult time working
its way around a big ego.

Lest you imagine otherwise,
what you think of yourself is not a secret.

> ## *A big ego is like an ugly tattoo; it's hard to hide.*

Self-centered people live in an anal universe.

A sure way to waste your day is to worry about what others think of you. Those others may be just as worried about what you think of them.

Humility is the proof in the pudding of the character of a person.

A hypocrite has a hard time fitting in because his ego takes up so much room.

You get shortchanged by saving all your love for yourself.

**Big egos have a way of
growing on little people.**

*Self-centered people don't realize
the small world they live in only
has room for a rear-view mirror.*

*When you look out only for yourself you are
blinded as to what other people see in you.*

> *"I learned a lesson about
> ego when I ran for governor of
> Arkansas. I approached a woman
> at a gas pump and said, 'Hi, my
> name is Hayes McClerkin and I'm
> running for governor.' She replied,
> 'What state?' That taught me to
> spell ego with a little e."*

*It is good to remember that others may not see
us in the light our egos make us think we look.*

*Most of our misery comes from worrying about
ourselves. This can be cured by helping others.*

A self-centered person can't stand change because it is a threat to what little she has.

A big ego and a full wheelbarrow have a lot in common. Both are difficult to maneuver.

If you are finding it difficult to get along with someone, try a little humility and a smile; they are free and they work wonders.

Self-centered people can't reach out to others, yet are puzzled by their lack of friends.

Self-centered people waste a lot of love on themselves that could better be shared with others.

Self-centered people have very small circles of friends, namely themselves.

A big ego has a hard time making friends.

Big egos are generally wedded to big mouths.

A big ego and bad breath have a lot in common; neither attracts a crowd.

Humility is a show of strength, not of weakness.

A caring person has the world for a view; a self-centered person has to settle for a mirror.

Put your ego on a diet, and you will look better in the eyes of others.

A big ego is a ticket to the top of "fool's hill."

When you compare yourself to others, your ego has taken control.

Egos are not fine wines; they don't get better with age.

A big ego is a difficult blemish to hide.

*It is difficult to be humble
if you think highly of yourself.*

**A self-centered person has
a difficult time defining love
because it involves others.**

*A person who likes to hear himself talk
is addressing a very small audience.*

*If you want to simplify your life,
learn how to spell ego with tiny letters.*

*Never forget that an out-of-control ego
will run over you before it hurts anyone else.*

Big egos usually don't have a heart to match.

A big ego never goes as far as a little humility.

Don't let your ego get over-inflated;
if you do you will drift away from your friends.

A person's pocketbook has a difficult time
keeping up with a big ego.

When your expectations in life are fueled
by your ego, you are running on empty.

A pocket full of money and a big ego,
when mixed, result in a fool.

It may be difficult to lose weight, but it is
even more so to reduce a big ego.

A person wrapped up in herself
is dealing with a tangled mess.

A big ego is how one sees himself,
but it doesn't reflect what is showing
to the rest of the world.

> # *A big ego is like a cow chip,*
> # *something to be side-stepped.*

It is OK to have an ego: just be sure
it is spelled with very small letters.

The amazing thing about a big ego is
how small a mind it takes to keep it blown up.

A big ego has a difficult time
solving small problems, and in time
they grow into big problems.

A big ego is like a runaway bus;
it misses a lot of stops along the road of life.

Conceit and bad breath have a lot in common;
they both turn people off.

A big ego will quickly turn pride into arrogance.

*A self-centered person leaves
very little for others to admire.*

*When you think only of yourself, you don't know
what other people may think of you.*

*Humility can open more doors
than a battering ram.*

*When you worry about what other people
think of you, all you do is feed your ego.*

*Never forget that an ego, once conceived,
creates a breeding ground for animosity.*

*If you don't look outside of yourself, you
will never enjoy the life going on around you.*

*For a self-centered person, life must be very
boring because the scenery never changes.*

*It is difficult to feel good about who you are if
you worry about what other people think of you.*

*Humility is not a show of weakness,
but evidence of strong character.*

*A person wrapped up in herself is
a package no one wants to open.*

*If you want to have a bad day, let your
self esteem turn into self-centeredness.*

A big ego is like a boomerang;
it can come back to haunt you.

*A self-dealing person is peddling
a cheap product.*

*If you want to live in a very small world,
think only of yourself.*

*It's interesting how a person with a high opinion
of herself is usually surrounded by people
who don't share that opinion.*

*It is difficult to receive admiration from others if
the most admired person in your life is yourself.*

*When you think more of others than you do
of yourself you are heart-healthy.*

*When you have more love for yourself
than you do for others, you are upside down
in your approach to life.*

Learning

"Learning is like rowing upstream.
As soon as you stop, you begin
drifting backwards."

Sowing the Seeds of Knowledge

My birthday was in December, too late to start school in September in the year in which I turned six. My mother didn't want me to be in the "low first" in the middle of the school year, so she enrolled me in a private school, Patty Hill. The school was small and run by Mrs. Patterson, who named it after some professor she had studied under at Columbia University.

Patty Hill was not exclusive. Mrs. Patterson was a Presbyterian, and her tithe to the church was to let the pastor's four children attend free. Others attended when their fathers painted the school building, which was an old house. Mrs. Patterson and one other teacher taught all six grades and kindergarten. The entire student body probably consisted of 30 to 40 children at any given time.

Every morning, regardless of grade, we were each expected to recite a Bible verse and give a current news event. I found that *Jesus Wept* saved me many a morning. We also had to study table manners, and on a Friday, once a month, we would give some sort of performance on the stage, which was located in the attic of the school.

Mrs. Patterson was a strict disciplinarian, and her punishment for almost any little infraction was to make us hold our hand out, whereby she would slap the palm with an eighteen-inch ruler. If we pulled back or flinched, she would slap the palm again. We soon learned to the accept punishment, mild though it was, for any misdeed.

Mrs. Patterson retired in 1943, and I was lucky enough to be in her last class, along with three other students of note. One was Fred Graham, who later reached fame as a television reporter and author. Another close friend, Ross Perot, also made a name for himself. The third, Bill Murphy, who became my closest friend in life, established a highly successful and profitable oil and gas drilling company.

Many other students from Patty Hill went on to successful careers, and in the early 1990s we all gathered and placed a public memorial to Mrs. Patterson. She was the rock upon which we all started our life journeys and an example of how one person can make a difference in the lives of others.

Thoughts About Learning

Not knowing is bad,
but not wanting to know is worse.

Education is like a drinking fountain;
some sip the water while others just gargle.

It is OK to ask for advice, but the
best expert on yourself is always you.

It is understandable to be wrong
but inexcusable to stay wrong.

We all learn by asking dumb questions.

If you want to learn the truth,
don't be afraid to ask tough questions.

The know-it-all misses out
on the joy of learning.

*Unfortunately, the human mind is like water;
you have to pump it to make it go uphill.*

*One of the best lessons to learn from a mistake
is that you may have to admit you made it.*

*The human mind needs an occasional
dose of sani-flush.*

You will never learn unless you ask.

*If you don't ask simple questions,
you may compound your ignorance.*

*Students who ask "why" will never learn
as much as those who ask "how."*

*Your mind isn't afraid of learning
unless you tell it otherwise.*

*Ask questions to solve problems,
not to create problems.*

*You sometimes learn more
by showing your ignorance.*

*If every lesson we learned was as successful
as toilet training we could wipe out illiteracy.*

*Ask "why" and you get an excuse;
ask "how" and you get an answer.*

**Sometimes the wisest thing a
person can say is "I don't know."**

*The bright side of a mistake, hopefully,
is that we learn to never make it again.*

Silence is golden because it hides ignorance.

*Don't be afraid to ask questions; that may be
the only way to prove you have a brain.*

*It is difficult to solve a problem
if you don't admit it exists.*

*Bull baffles brains 90 percent of the time.
Let's make sure we use the remaining
10 percent wisely.*

*The student who knows all the answers
will never be as smart as the student
asking the questions.*

*Mind over matter has particular
importance in a barnyard.*

*Straight answers will take
the curves out of problems.*

*A closed mind is like a rock;
an open mind is like a sponge.*

*A wise person shares the lessons
she learns from the mistakes she makes.*

*Your problems only get larger if you wait
for someone else to solve them.*

*It isn't what you learned in school that counts;
it is how you use what you learned
that matters in the real world.*

*To have a full life, you have to keep
filling your tank of knowledge.*

*The learning curve on your mistakes is steep
if you can't admit you made them.*

Common sense comes in handy when you run out of education.

A fool knows all; a wise man seeks to learn all.

*The more time you spend telling people
how much you know lessens the time
you have to prove it.*

*A roadblock to solving a problem could be
that you are part of the problem.*

*If you keep asking "why," you will never
get around to learning "how."*

*Most people who think they know it all
actually have a lot to learn.*

*Most "know it all's" talk themselves
to the back of the class.*

*Large problems are often created
by ignoring small problems.*

*If you look at a problem as a challenge,
you will find a solution.*

*A man's mind can be his castle
only if he lets knowledge in.*

Positive thinking is the toilet paper of the mind.

*Experience is a tough teacher, one
who gives the test first, then the lesson.*

*If you are in over your head,
make the condition temporary
by asking questions and finding answers.*

*Teaching by example is difficult because
we have to do what we say.*

*The smart man knows when to sit, listen, and
learn while the fool in the seat beside him
stands and speaks.*

*An important lesson to learn is to never
overestimate the level of your ability or
underestimate the gravity of a problem.*

*When you meet a know-it-all,
you have just met a slow learner.*

*If you take the time to listen to the
"know it all," you soon learn that
he knows a lot about very little.*

*Never forget that you can always learn
new things from old friends.*

*When you teach with words, you make a
statement; when you teach by example,
you make a difference.*

*A person who is absolutely certain
about everything she says may be
trying to hide her ignorance.*

*If you want an exciting life,
make every day a learning experience.*

*You can never learn from a mistake
if you don't admit you made one.*

*Many wise men talk themselves
into ignorance.*

*A person who has to tell you how smart he is
wears his ignorance on his shirt sleeve.*

People who think they know it all have a lot to learn, and much of it is about themselves.

Know-it-alls never listen; therefore they never learn.

Don't let your pride stop you from asking questions; to do otherwise is to compound your ignorance.

One thing the know-it-all doesn't know is how little she has to offer.

The fool who thinks he knows it all could take a lesson from the wise man asking all the questions.

Money

⌘

*"Those who think money makes a person
generally get short-changed in life."*

The Value of Money

A s a small child, my parents tried to teach me the value of money. I remember when I was about eight or nine years old, I received 25 cents every Saturday morning as my allowance. Five cents of this had to be put in the plate at Sunday School, and the rest was mine to spend.

In those days, it was safe for a child to travel around Texarkana, and each Saturday morning, my friend Bubby from across the street—who was two years older—and I would catch the bus and go to the Strand movie house downtown. It cost a nickel for two bus tokens that would get us to town and back, and the double feature cowboy movie, with serial thrown in, cost another nickel. That left me with a dime to spend on popcorn, caps for my cap pistol, or whatever else 10 cents could buy. I shopped wisely with that dime.

If I could catch my father at Johnson's Drug Store, down the street from the movie, I could save a bus token and catch a ride back home. He and his friends liked to meet on Saturday mornings and drink in the back of the store. I had some hairy rides home, just to save a bus token.

Money took another track when I started practicing law. I had a senior law partner, Willis B. Smith, who went by the nickname of Jug. He was my mentor and one of those fine people we meet rarely in life who makes a difference. Jug told me many times,

"Hayes, if you practice good law, good money will follow, but if you practice for money all you will get is bad law."

How true.

Thoughts on Money

*One who lives in anticipation
of an inheritance will die broke.*

⌘

*Fortune may buy fame, but if you want
respect to go along with it, you must earn it.*

⌘

*People who use money to impress others
end up with empty pockets.*

⌘

*A person who equates happiness to only
money is swimming in a shallow river.*

⌘

*Lasting love is hard to find when
you wrap it up with dollar signs.*

⌘

*Money will only make you truly happy
when you do something good with it.*

⌘

Stingy people have few friends, if any.

⌘

Stingy people get out of life what they give.

⌘

*Most people don't appreciate what
they have until they have lost it.*

⌘

*Anyone who has to use money to make a
statement has a very small vocabulary.*

⌘

*Have you noticed that the only friends a stingy
person has are those who were bought?*

⌘

*People who like to buy acceptance are not
afraid to use someone else's money.*

⌘

*When money talks, the ones who listen
don't know it, but they have just joined
the world's oldest profession.*

⌘

*Kind words are free,
and they will gain you more happiness
than you can ever buy with money.*

**If money is your only source of happiness,
your soul is for sale.**

✽

*Someone who puts money first
will come in second in the race of life.*

✽

*Arrogance and money always seem to mix
but will never win a popularity contest.*

✽

*The quickest road to poverty is trying
to find a way to buy happiness.*

✽

*People can't bury a bad past with money,
but they can overcome it with character.*

✽

*When you only look at what other people have,
you fail to see all the treasures you have.*

✽

*If all you want is what someone else has,
you will never have anything of your own.*

✽

*When we get wrapped up in what we don't
have, we fail to unpack the blessings we have.*

✽

⌘

Cheap people are like cheap underwear;
they wear thin quick.

⌘

> ## Stingy people are unhappy people because they get out of life what they give.

⌘

If you buy social acceptance with money,
it doesn't have much value.

⌘

Before you can buy respect, you first have to
find someone willing to sell it.

⌘

Buying social acceptance is fleeting fancy
because there is always someone
waiting to outbid you.

⌘

A person who earns respect gets to keep it,
but a person who buys respect only gets to
keep it until someone else purchases it.

⌘

Gifts that come from the pocket and not from the heart take all the joy out of giving.

⌘

Cheap people and cheap suits have one thing in common: neither wears well.

⌘

If you have to use money to impress people, you may not realize it, but you are morally broke.

⌘

If money is the only music to your ears, you are tone deaf.

⌘

Fame bought is fleeting; fame earned is enduring.

⌘

When you buy happiness, you are dealing in used goods.

⌘

*It is easy to buy acceptance,
but when you do, you have just engaged
in the world's oldest profession.*

⌘

Love, not money, is the currency for marriage.

⌘

*Giving money with strings attached
is like playing with a yo-yo.*

⌘

*When you buy friends, you always
have to worry about inflation.*

⌘

*People who have to buy the friendship of
others don't know the meaning of self-respect.*

⌘

*If you have to spend money to make a
statement, you don't have much to talk about.*

⌘

*Bought happiness is like discount deodorant;
it doesn't last very long.*

⌘

*If money is your best friend,
you are leading a lonely life.*

118

**If money is your only friend,
save enough to pay your pallbearers.**

⌘

*When all you do to gain respect
is spend money, the only person
you are fooling is yourself.*

⌘

*It is difficult to get people to admire you
when your idea of hard work is
claiming an inheritance.*

⌘

*If you have to buy social acceptance, you have
a good chance of ending up morally broke.*

⌘

*Money may get you where you are going,
but only perseverance keeps you there.*

⌘

*Bought respect is like jello on hot street;
it melts fast and leaves a sticky mess.*

⌘

*People who think they can buy
social acceptance will never discover
their true worth in life.*

⌘

Leadership

*"A good leader knows
it is not who created the problem
that is important;
it is how to solve it that matters."*

Lessons in Leadership

During my stint in the U.S. Navy in the latter part of and immediately following the Korean Conflict, I found myself as navigator aboard an attack transport, the USS *Chilton* (APA-38). This was a strange responsibility for a kid from Arkansas who had never been aboard a ship until reporting to the *Chilton*.

In port, there wasn't much for the navigator to do since we were tied up to a pier. I took advantage of the circumstances, and after officer's call every morning, I would "hit the bunk" again and try to rescue myself from the night before at the officer's club.

The men in my department started to kid me about being *navigator in port*. The chief petty officer and lead petty officer came to me with an idea. They suggested that each day we were in port, we should designate a different man in the department as *navigator in port*. That person would be relieved of duty for the day. I would get his liberty card from the master at arms, and he could do as he wanted.

I approved the idea—which was not quite up to regulation—with one stipulation. The person designated as *navigator in port* had to have someone in the department ready to perform his duties if the need arose. This unknowingly created a situation of cross training.

The idea was a big hit, and morale went sky high. After a few weeks, the executive officer, a stickler for regulations, got wind of the scheme and put a stop to it. He was already not the most popular man on the ship, and this didn't help his reputation.

Sometime thereafter, we were in Guantanamo Bay, Cuba, for refresher training. Many of the drills were simulated combat situations with people being taken out of action. The crew of the navigation department excelled because of the cross training they had voluntarily undertaken in support of the *navigator in port* scheme.

The navigation department received the highest grades of any for our type ship in the Atlantic Fleet for that year. The captain commended me for my leadership, and I never had the moral urge to tell him that it all came about because I was sleeping off hangovers when in port. But, I did give all the credit to the men of the navigation department.

From this I learned several lessons in leadership that have lasted a lifetime. First, success has a lot to do with circumstance and luck. Second, don't take advantage of those for whom you are responsible. And finally, if you have good people, let them perform.

Thoughts on Leadership

*When leaders begin to think they are
indispensable, others start thinking
it's time for fresh ideas and new blood.*

Good leaders substitute planning for worry.

*Leaders know that a good way to stumble
is to compare themselves to others.*

*Skippers who want to steer and never paddle,
often find themselves alone in the boat.*

*The business leader who likes to run everything
generally runs off those around him.*

*Supervisors who try to control everyone
can't figure out why they are never accepted.*

*Master builders know a strong wall
is made of many small bricks.*

*The character of a leader is determined
by how he treats his followers.*

*The more a person in authority thinks of
himself, the less others will look up to him.*

*A good shepherd leads by kindness,
not intimidation.*

*A leader who throws his weight around
will always be viewed as a lightweight.*

*When a supervisor begins to think he is right
all the time, he has just made his first mistake.*

*When leaders overestimate their ability,
they underestimate what others think of them.*

*Leaders don't let what they cannot do
interfere with what they can do.*

Good leaders seek respect over popularity.

*True leaders recognize and respect
what others take pride in.*

*Leaders know it is all right to be wrong
once in a while but a disaster to stay wrong.*

*Business leaders get to the top
by asking questions.*

*True leaders know the words "I'm sorry"
solve many world problems.*

*Leaders stand out because they are
not afraid to go against the crowd.*

*Those who contribute the least, generally
complain the most about leadership.*

Leaders don't mountain climb over anthills.

*Good leaders know it is not a waste of time
to seek perfection.*

*Leaders know that wishful thinking
and risk assessment should not
be done at the same time.*

*Leadership is like a football game.
You have to play your best to stay ahead.*

*Leadership is not a straight road. You have to
turn the corners to find the opportunities.*

*Following the same path every day
will not a leader make.*

***Following the crowd will only
get you where everyone else is
going. It won't put you in front.***

*Respected leaders judge themselves by
the same standards that they set for others.*

*Leaders recognize it only takes one idea
or one person to make a difference in life.*

*Leaders don't worry about what they can't do;
they concentrate on what they can do.*

Leaders are not copycats.

*True leadership is the ability to give,
not the need to take.*

Leaders ask "how," not "why."

*Leaders make a difference in this world
by adding, not subtracting.*

Indecision is not the mark of leadership.

*Ironically, we sometimes come in first
by putting ourselves last.*

*Leaders don't solve problems
by blaming others.*

**Leaders are not afraid of life.
They challenge it every day.**

Leaders ask questions to solve problems,
not to create problems.

Leadership is achieved when
you don't overestimate yourself
and you don't underestimate others.

Lack of leadership is rooted in indecision.

If you follow a trail, you will
only go where others have been.

Pioneers know the limits to life can be
reached only when you try to exceed them.

Great leaders don't do great things;
they do the right things.

*To be a leader, you must be able
to accept and admit mistakes.*

*A leader who abuses power
will eventually be overpowered.*

An overbearing leader is lighter than he thinks.

**Leaders know that big ideas are
best developed with small steps.**

*Leaders who downplay their own importance
go up in the eyes of followers.*

*Everyone wants the glory,
but good trailblazers have the guts.*

*Fear of the unknown has never
solved a problem or stopped an explorer.*

130

*A good leader knows when to guide and when
to follow, and when to pull and when to push.*

*Words are forgotten; actions are remembered.
So, lead by doing and keep your mouth shut.*

*A trailblazer knows that a sure way
to get lost is to start cutting corners.*

*To be a leader in life, you must contribute
more to the universe than you take out.*

*A so-called leader who looks down on others
doesn't stand very tall in the eyes of followers.*

*How far a leader goes in life depends on his
ability to get other people to give him a push.*

Innovative leaders are decision-makers.

*Great inventors are not afraid to challenge
what others say as the truth.*

131

*The leader who wants to steer and never
paddle may find himself alone in the boat.*

If all you do is try to keep up with someone else, you will always follow and never lead.

If you think leadership is a straight road, you will come to a dead end fast.

When you follow a well-marked trail, all you will find are the candy wrappers of those who have gone before you.

So-called leaders who find it easy to proclaim what is wrong with the world have a hard time realizing they are part of the problem.

A wise leader shares what he learns from the mistakes he makes.

The person who knows all the answers will never catch the leader who asks all the questions.

Leaders know that getting started is easy; staying motivated through the long haul is the difficult part.

You will never get out in front if your focus is on where everyone else is going.

*The best way to get nowhere in life
is to follow the crowd.*

Leadership looks easy until you assume it.

*Looking down on others is not the way
for leaders to be looked up to.*

*Unless he keeps moving in life, a leader
will soon find himself behind the times.*

*The best way for a leader to lose her way on
the road of life is to start making assumptions.*

Leaders don't play "what If?"

*A higher-up who looks down on others
exposes his backside for all to look up to.*

*Life can take many directions,
but a good guide has a compass.*

*An explorer is always looking for new hills
to climb and new territory to conquer.*

*We all have baggage in our lives;
leaders just carry it better than others.*

*A leader knows that problems are difficult
to solve if you don't admit they exist.*

*When two people differ, a real leader
tries to balance the difference.*

*Innovative leaders know that
if you don't improve on today's success,
you are looking at tomorrow's failure.*

The unknown is a challenge, not a fear,
to a born explorer.

If you just want to be like someone else,
you will never be a leader.

How far a leader will go for others has
a great bearing on long he will stay in front.

Leaders know that large problems are
usually created by ignoring small ones.

A leader without a vision is like
an ostrich with its head in the
sand and its rear end showing.

A social climber will never be the lead dog.

Leadership means not
comparing yourself to others.

**The only road map on the path
to leadership is the one you draw.**

*Good leaders don't excuse bad decisions
by calling them bad luck.*

*Innovative leaders know that If you look at a
problem as a challenge you will find a solution.*

*Mistakes are part of life. How one reacts
to them determines leadership ability.*

*Leadership ability can be compared
to a "Y" in the road of life. The
downhill choice usually is a dead end.*

*Life is full of problems. Finding solutions
is the key to innovative leadership.*

*The true leader knows the difference
between bad judgment and bad luck.*

***Heros happen; leaders are born.
You can be both by practicing
random acts of kindness.***

*A leader is on Lonely Street if he thinks
his way is the only way.*

*Good soldiers don't let fear immobilize.
They only permit it to create caution.*

*The successful leader uses the word include;
the arrogant leader only knows exclude.*

*If all you want in life is to be like someone else,
you will never lead; you will always end up
in second place.*

*Great generals know that fear instills caution,
but fear of fear causes debilitation.*

*It is not how one thinks, but how one acts out
his thoughts that creates the image of a leader.*

*If your life is in a rut, it may be
from walking the same path every day.
Become a leader and blaze new trails.*

*Indecision creates what some people define
as bad luck and others call poor leadership.*

*A true leader never falls behind
in putting other people first.*

*True leaders define their surroundings;
followers let their surroundings define them.*

*The character of a leader is determined by
whether she admits a mistake or covers it up.*

*Innovative leaders know that more mistakes in
life are made by inaction than by wrong action.*

*People who lead with their hearts never
have to ask directions on the road of life.*

*It is rare to find big talkers and big doers
in the same person. The latter are leaders;
the former want to be.*

*It is hard to lead if you don't know
where you want to go.*

*Most bad breaks in a chain of command
are caused by poor leadership.*

Leadership means filling the cup of life until it runneth over.

*A wise man leads with his heart,
a fool with his mouth.*

*The one constant in life is change,
and many fall behind for fear of facing it.*

*It is hard to come in first if all you want
to do is make the team.*

*Beware of leaders who want
to control rather than serve.*

A good leader is pro-active, not reactive.

*A business leader who keeps past mistakes
on his mind is making a corporate mistake.*

*The person who says "we" leads
while the person who says "I" wonders
why he is always in second place.*

*Leaders who try to run everything
usually wind up running their followers off.*

*The leader who lets caution turn to fear
is flirting with failure.*

*A powerful leader knows that the
worst enemy of good ideas is fear of risk.*

*A true leader will never regret doing
the right thing, even if he has to admit
to being wrong to do so.*

*If there are no skid marks on your road to
leadership, it means you haven't gone very far.*

It is easy to follow; the challenge arises
when you get to the head of the line.

The person who knows it all will never catch
the innovator asking all the questions.

Leaders who downplay their own importance
go up in the eyes of others.

True admiration follows the boss who
finds fault in himself before criticizing others.

*"The crew of the navigation
department excelled because
of the cross training they had
voluntarily undertaken in support
of the 'navigator in port' scheme.
The captain commended me for
my leadership, and I never had the
moral urge to tell him that it all
came about because I was sleeping
off hangovers when in port."*

*A leader will never be a has-been
if he keeps a can-do attitude.*

*If you are facing a sea of problems,
take the plunge by asking questions
and finding answers.*

*Great communicators know that if you want
people to listen to what you have to say,
don't let your mouth outrun your brain.*

*Good leaders know that luck, bad or good,
is usually created by your own actions.*

*Respected leaders are not afraid
to admit they are wrong. It is a tribute
to their self-confidence.*

*True admiration comes to those who want to do
something that lasts longer than themselves.*

*The person who waits for things to happen
in life will never understand why she
always ends up in second place.*

144

*The ability to lead is determined
a great deal by the ability to decide.*

*The best way to fall behind in life
is to rest on your laurels.*

*Leadership ability means never
underestimating the power of a smile.*

*Leaders don't let the "ifs" in life distract
from the possibilities for the future.*

*Fear debilitates; faith builds.
Don't make it a difficult choice.*

Dignity

*"We are all different,
but our respect for
the dignity of everyone
should be equal."*

Defining Dignity

As a child growing up during the Depression, I was fortunate that my father had a fairly good job for the times. He was the secretary-treasurer of a wholesale hardware company. It provided a good living but not a lot of luxuries. We lived in a small five room house and the pavement ended about one hundred feet from our front door. It was a wonderful place to grow up because all the elements of nature and civilization were nearby.

Somewhat unusual for our circumstances was the fact that we had a black woman, Dossie Coleman, as our maid, plus Dossie's daughter, Adee, and her two sons, Cleo and John, helping around the house. Adee helped Dossie inside. Cleo was part-time yard man and baby sitter and also taught me all the curse words in the book, which resulted in my having a great deal of soap put on my tongue. John was our driver, a necessity because my father was prone to drink. John's driving saved our lives in a terrible auto wreck.

Dossie and her children were a part of my life and I thought little of it at the time. Years later, I asked my mother why we had so many people working in and around our small house. She said that Dossie's husband, Horton, worked at the hardware company and that my father knew that they were having a difficult time financially. He put them to work around the house for a dollar a day, knowing that otherwise they would have to borrow money to live. This afforded them the dignity of earning money as opposed to begging for it.

One evening, my father got up from the dinner table, took a few steps, and died unexpectedly from a heart attack. I was ten years old at the time and an only child. My father's funeral was in the old southern tradition. His body and casket were brought into the living room of our small home. Mother and I sat and greeted friends as they came to pay their respects and view the body. At about four or five o'clock in the afternoon, it was time for the blacks to come and pay their respects. They all came, dressed in their finest, and to a person, Horton, Dossie, Adee, Cleo, and John, leaned over and kissed my father in the casket, and all left crying.

I didn't realize it at the time, but I had just witnessed my first, and probably best, example of dignity and respect I would experience in my lifetime.

Thoughts About Dignity

*Respect is a short word to say, but
by showing it we can all go a long way.*

*Earn respect and it is yours; buy respect and
it is yours until someone offers a higher price.*

*Real strength of character is defined by
who you lift rather than by how much you lift.*

*The worth of a man is determined
by how he treats other people.*

*The best way to gain respect is to
show respect for others less fortunate.*

*Respect for others is a great investment.
It costs nothing and pays great dividends.*

*Showing respect for others doesn't cost a cent,
yet we sometimes hoard it like it is gold.*

*How you treat your fellow man depends
a great deal on how you define dignity.*

*It is difficult to respect the person
who lacks respect for others.*

*Respect can take a lifetime to be earned,
but it can be lost in a second.*

*If you don't respect the dignity of others,
at least keep your feelings to yourself.*

*Respect is earned by placing the feelings
of others before yourself.*

*Your dignity is defined by how you look in
the eyes of others, not how you see yourself.*

*When you try to buy respect, you are flirting
with the world's oldest profession.*

*Don't let your quest for respect
rob you of your dignity.*

*The dignity you afford others depends
a great deal on respecting yourself first.*

*Friends are cultivated with mutual respect
and compassion.*

Recognize and respect the dignity of others.

*Seek respect rather than popularity;
it lasts longer.*

*Very few people have true friendships because
they require sacrifice and mutual respect,
attributes that don't come easy.*

**Harsh words hurt; kind words
heal wounds and build dignity.**

*Being respectful doesn't cost a cent,
and it is a good way to start each day.*

*Never pass up an opportunity
to respect another's privacy, even if
you have to leave them alone to do it.*

*When you speak, say something
that will make the listener feel good.*

*The best way to deal with a disrespectful
person is to not respond in kind.*

*Kind words and respectful actions
leave lasting impressions.*

*If you want to have a good day,
start it off with kindness and respect.*

*A man shows character by treating with respect
someone who cannot help him in any way.*

*True character is the ability
to be respectful in all circumstances.*

Respectful behavior is contagious.
Don't be afraid to spread it around.

Disrespectful people have few friends, if any.

Disrespectful people get out of life
exactly what they give.

Great people don't do great things,
they do the right and respectful things.

If you must judge a person,
judge her on how she treats other people.

Always open a conversation
with a smile and show of respect.

When you buy respect, people resent you;
when you earn respect, people admire you.

154

*Never let a day end without saying
a kind word and doing a good deed.*

*Kind words build dignity and will gain you
more respect than you can ever buy.*

*People who try to buy respect and prestige
are only impressing themselves.*

*A sure way to gain respect is to act out
your convictions, not talk about them.*

*To get respect, you have to add to,
not take from, society.*

*The best way to be a big person is to
show respect for the dignity of little people.*

*Never underestimate the power of a smile
or a show of respect.*

The best diet for a heavy heart
is one rich in love and respect.

*Respect is strange; it's wonderful to receive,
but not so easy to give.*

*To have meaning in your life, show
more respect than you hope to gain.*

*Investing in the dignity of others costs nothing,
but pays great dividends.*

*A person who gives to gain respect
isn't giving enough.*

*Being respectful can make a big difference
in another person's life.*

*A sure way to find happiness
is to show respect.*

*You will win more friends with acts of kindness
and respect than you will with words.*

*If you want a healthy heart, show kindness and
respect to someone who can't help you.*

Kind words can restore lost dignity.

*Life is a pleasure when you respect
the dignity of those below you rather than
envy the wealth of those above you.*

*"When I was growing up,
Dossie was our maid, and her
children did odd jobs around the
house. One day I asked my mother
why we had so many people
working around our small house.
She told me that my father was
lucky enough to have a job during
the Depression, and instead of
lending Dossie's children money
they couldn't repay, he gave them
the dignity of earning it."*

*You have to earn self-respect, and in doing so,
you gain the respect of others.*

*Respect is gained by what you give,
not what you take out of life.*

Mutual respect is the formula for friendship.

*Being polite and respectful saves time;
you don't have to apologize later.*

*The best way to make friends is to
be respectful in all circumstances.*

*Respect is a win-win situation.
Give it and you earn it in return.*

*Dignity, once lost, is difficult to regain.
Don't be the cause.*

*It is difficult to be respectful of others
if you don't like yourself.*

Respect is easy to say until you have to show it.

159

*The best diet for a heavy heart is
a good dose of love and respect.*

Good words are forgotten; good intentions
often remain undone; but, good deeds
are etched in memories.

You will be a better person if you look at others
with love and respect rather than envy or hate.

Buy respect and you have to worry about
inflation; earn it and it is always on the rise.

Showing compassion and respect for your
fellow man will put real meaning in your life.

People who buy respect will never know
the good feelings they have missed
in life by not earning it.

*People who buy respect don't know
the meaning of dignity.*

*Don't be near-sighted when it comes
to showing respect for others.*

*When all you do to gain respect is spend
money, the only one you are fooling is yourself.*

*It is difficult to respect someone
who shows no respect for others.*

*A person who has to buy respect and a streaker
have a lot in common. Think about it.*

*Show respect for what others have done for
you, and you will gain respect for yourself.*

*If you want to get hooked on tranquilizers,
try a dose of kindness and respect.*

*Humility and respectfulness are the proof in
the pudding of the character of a person.*

*A wise person will instill dignity in others
with kind words and good deeds.*

*Kind words are more effective
if accompanied by kind deeds.*

*A kind word to a stranger can make a difference
in his life and it will do wonders for yours.*

It is never out of style to be kind to our fellow man.

*Kind words are meaningless
unless accompanied by respect.*

*It takes effort to love and respect everybody,
and it's all too easy to get lazy in that regard.*

When you buy respect,
you are dealing in used goods.

*Self-respect is a show
of strength and character.*

*Character is more than a word;
it is defined by acts of kindness and respect.*

*It's difficult to have compassion and respect
for people who feel sorry for themselves.*

*Good thoughts are worthless unless
they become good deeds.*

You don't earn respect by showing disrespect.

*If you buy respect, you have a good chance
of ending up morally broke.*

**We all admire people who have
the strength of character to laugh
at themselves before they
poke fun at others.**

> ## *Kind words will always catch a disrespectful person off guard.*

Never forget in dealing with people that there is a fine line between resentment and respect.

Never forget that when you show respect, you can make a bad day bright for someone else.

Being respectful can open more doors than a battering ram.

It is difficult to stumble on the road of life if your path is paved with respect for others.

Integrity has a hard time coping with disrespect.

You will never enjoy the riches of life if you are stingy with respect for the dignity of others.

Arrogance

*"A self-important person
actually plays but a minor role
in the big picture of life."*

A Case of a Two-Legged Jackass

The straw that broke the camel's back in my many years of practicing law was a client who possessed neither humility nor a belief that he was wrong. I had been practicing in the field of oil and gas law, and in the latter years of practice, I found myself representing a so-called oil and gas tycoon. He insisted that a law suit be filed against someone just like him. I resisted, but at the urging of an out-of-state lawyer, I finally relented.

The suit was filed, and a jury trial was set. I soon discovered that trial preparation was beneath my client because he had "a good lawyer to take care of it." By now, it was too late for me to back out. The client showed up for "trial preparation" at 6:30 in the morning of the day the trial was to begin at 8:30.

It soon became obvious that I was representing the worst of two liars. During the trial, I must admit, I relied solely on my instincts. I remarked to the presiding judge during a recess that this trial was going to have the same ending for my client as that of a one-legged bootlegger whom I had been court appointed to defend early in my career. I told the judge the only defense I had in the bootlegger case was that the officers found no crutch marks at the location of the illegal still. It didn't work.

After the trial of the oil and gas tycoon, which also turned out against my client, the judge told me that my analysis of the probable result was right. My client became furious at me, never realizing that his own arrogance determined the outcome. Not only had he declined to assist in the preparation of his trial, but he also was not credible on the stand.

This experience, coupled with some other factors, made me realize that practicing law was no longer fun, and it was time to become *"of counsel."* All that arrogance accomplishes is the two-legged jackass it creates and the trail of resentment and distrust it leaves in its wake.

Thoughts on Arrogance

General "Vinegar Joe" Stilwell told his troops during World War II, "The higher a monkey climbs the pole, the more people can see his ass when he shows it."

Humility never wears thin to those around you.

A wise man will always lead a wise ass.

We have to brush away bad breath, and we also have to brush up on correcting bad manners.

The only difference between an arrogant person and a jackass is two legs.

A two-legged jackass is conceived by crossing arrogance and a big ego.

Sometimes it is difficult to cover your tail when your mouth is open.

*Arrogance and money always seem to mix
but will never be the perfect couple.*

An arrogant person travels in a small circle.

*Envy and overbearing pride are a recipe
for self-destruction.*

*Just because a man has his pants on
doesn't mean he can't show his butt.*

*If you have to tell people how important
you are, you don't have much to talk about.*

*People will not know you are a jackass
until you start acting like one.*

*The best way to stick your foot in your mouth
is to open it.*

*It's funny how people who claim to be big shots
never seem to pull the trigger at the right time.*

171

The person who flies by the seat of his pants, could wind up showing his butt.

Self-important people traveling the road of life see only what is in their rear-view mirror.

Politicians and helium balloons have a lot in common: both are kept flying with hot air.

Arrogance and ego will blind you to reality and lead to failure.

If you get wrapped up in your own importance, you may be the only present under the tree.

A wise man looks in his own rear-view mirror before he calls someone else a jackass.

*The talent in a person is often wasted
when she becomes self–important.*

*Most people who claim to have it made
lead with their backside.*

*Swallowing your pride, like taking castor oil,
is hard to do, but generally has good results.*

*A smart ass is found on two legs
more often than four.*

*Pride can be a positive attribute until it
gets in the way of common sense.*

*Self-important people are very nearsighted and
thereby miss a lot of the beauty around them.*

*If you allow success to become self-
importance, your backside will begin to show.*

It is hard to keep high hopes up with hot air.

It doesn't take much to be a fool,
and it takes even less to fool a fool.

The best way to create a two-legged jackass
is with an open mouth.

Never forget that others may interpret
your pride as arrogance.

A big mouth often exposes a small mind.

Before you start to brag, remember you are
about to say something no one wants to hear.

Arrogance is fine as long as
you keep it to yourself.

If you have to talk about yourself, at least
make it something people can laugh about.

It is easy to be a fool;
the difficult part is admitting it.

It is hard to kick a moving ass.

175

*It is unusual for a braggart to get through life
without being thought a fool.*

*Arrogance is hard to hide
once a braggart opens his mouth.*

> **Arrogance and greed can cloud
> kindness and good deeds but
> can never overshadow them.**

*God created four-legged jackasses;
man makes the two-legged variety.*

*A person wrapped up in his own importance
lives in a very small box.*

*Arrogance and bad breath have a lot
in common: people try to avoid both.*

Braggarts have to live by their imagination.

*You show class when you apologize for your
errors; you show your backside when you don't.*

*The best friend an arrogant person
will ever have is his mirror.*

*The end result of an open mouth
and closed mind is arrogance.*

*A self-important person can't stand change
because it is a threat to what little he has.*

It is hard to recognize a fool if you are the fool.

*The best way to be labeled a fool is to try
and cover ignorance with arrogance.*

*Self-important people don't realize that
the tight circle they live in only gives them
a view of their own rear end.*

*Handle pride with care. When mixed with ego
it can quickly turn into arrogance.*

*When you breed greed with arrogance,
you get illegitimate offspring.*

*Since it is often difficult to keep the mouth
and brain in step, it's best to let the brain lead.*

*The high opinion you have of yourself
generally leaves your rear end exposed.*

> ### *If you want to lose your way on the road of life, take the path of self-importance.*

*Self-esteem can be mistaken for arrogance,
so take care how you express it.*

*A person who leads with his heart will have
more friends and admirers than the person
who leads with his mouth.*

*It is difficult to be humble
if you think too highly of yourself.*

*A person who likes to hear herself talk
is addressing a very small audience.*

**The arrogant person says "I"
and stands alone. Smart people
say "we" and stand united.**

*If we let our pride get over-inflated,
we will soon find our friends drifting away.*

*Bragging will always distort any positive
opinion others may have of you.*

*If you have to brag about what you have,
people don't envy you; they recognize
the small world you live in.*

A closed mouth is the best disguise a fool has.

Arrogant people and cheap suits have
something in common: neither wears well.

*When we get wrapped up in our own
importance, most people laugh at the package.*

It is hard to hide a fool behind a big mouth.

*If you have to brag to feel good, people won't
admire you; they'll avoid you like the plague.*

*An arrogant person is like a cow chip,
something to be avoided.*

*A fool tries to impress with bragging; a
wise man communicates with positive actions.*

*A truly big person takes the time
to help little people.*

*Ironically, people who downplay their
own importance go up in the eyes of others.*

*The more you boast about yourself,
the less others will be impressed with you.*

A person who takes pride in what he gives is respected; a person who shows pride in what he has accumulated is not.

Arrogance leaves little for others to admire.

Humility can open more doors than the battering ram of arrogance.

Since bragging and humility don't mix, choose the latter. It makes life easier.

A person who is arrogant about his wisdom is actually showing his ignorance.

Arrogance will never win you a popularity contest.

When self-confidence becomes over-confidence, you can be sure, you are on the road to arrogance.

*It is difficult to be around someone
covered in overbearing pride.*

Never forget that arrogance is a self-inflicted wound.

*Resentment is the by-product of arrogance;
friendship is the offspring of humility.*

*A self-important person has a hard time seeing
all the beauty in others that surrounds her.*

*Humility is not a show of weakness,
but rather evidence of strong character.*

*Self-esteem turned self-importance
is the formula for a bad day.*

*When you act like you are better than
everyone else, you are only fooling yourself.*

*The sad thing about braggarts is
they believe what they say.*

*If you want people to laugh at you,
keep bragging; if you want people
to befriend you, keep smiling.*

*Never forget that humility is attractive;
arrogance is avoided.*

***A self-dealing person is
peddling a cheap product.***

*A man with a high opinion of himself
is frequently surrounded by people
who don't share that opinion.*

Life

"Life's best-kept secret is simple.
If you want a heavy burden,
practice hate;
if you want to experience joy,
spread love."

Getting the Most Out of Life

When we are growing up, we don't fully understand the mind set we are developing by what is going on around us. I have always said that I grew up in a neighborhood where the pavement stopped. This provided an environment where the imagination could go wild.

When I was a child, families didn't have televisions or computer games. We had books to read, we had radios to listen to, and we had our imaginations. I look back and find it difficult to imagine that we thought rolling an old tire down the street with a stick was fun. But it was because we made it so.

By "we," I am referring to my friends Bubby and Davis. Bubby was a couple of years older than I, and if I had to liken him to a well-known personality, it would be Huck Finn. He was the ring leader and taught us how to use our imaginations. We actually thought we could dig to China, and we tried for days. We also always believed we would have succeeded if the postman hadn't fallen into the hole.

Street-savvy Bubby led us to the monument business in town, where we would pick up pieces of marble and granite, then try our best to make arrow heads for our homemade bows and arrows. We made scooters out of two-by-fours and roller skates. We played in our tree house with mystical figures we made up in our minds.

Geographically, our world was very small, but in

our minds it was larger than life. It had minnows in the creek and fresh tar in the cracks of the street that we could cut out and chew. What else did a young mind need?

What does all this mean in the scheme of life? Maybe a good background on which to build. Davis took his imagination and went on to become a very successful businessman. Bubby took his wits into the ownership of a truck dealership. And, I can trace whatever successes I've had in life back to my roots and the lessons I learned alongside my friends in the neighborhood where the pavement stopped.

Bubby died a few years ago of cancer. When he was diagnosed, I was out of town, and he called to tell me the news. I immediately drove home. We went directly to the old neighborhood and walked the streets and alleys. The place that once loomed larger than life itself now seemed so small. But, it still held our memories, and together we hugged, laughed, and cried.

Thoughts About Life

*Life is not what you make it, but what
you get out of what you make.*

*Life is like a yo-yo, with lots of ups and downs.
Be ever careful not to let the string break.*

*Many good things in life are hidden in
unusual places. It's up to us so seek and find.*

*There is much more to life than waking up
in the morning and going to bed at night.*

*Life is like driving a car. Just stay the course
and don't worry about the next curve
until you get there.*

*Our quality of life is like a bucket of water. It
will evaporate if we don't continually add to it.*

Of all the angles in life, take the right angle.

Life is not a straight road. We have to turn the corners to find the opportunities.

It is difficult to stumble on the road of life if you remain humble.

Life will be very boring if you are afraid to lose.

Life is like rowing upstream. If you give up you go backwards.

Life is like a reading a book. You have to turn all the pages to enjoy the plot.

Life is like walking through a cow pasture. You better watch your step.

Life has a paddle that fits everyone's butt, and it hurts when it hits.

Life is too short to look back.

The path of life will be much straighter if you don't have to step around your ego all the time.

It only takes one idea or one person to make a difference in your life.

Life is a lot like a book. It often starts out slow but toward the end feels like someone is speed-reading.

If life was meant to be more than one day at a time, we wouldn't need sunsets.

Life may not be the easiest job in town, but it is one we all have to work at.

If you think your life has a lot in common with a diaper, it's time to change it.

190

Life is too short to be around unhappy people.

The limits to your life can be known
only when you try to exceed them.

It is not a detour on the road of life
to go out of your way to help someone.

Life is not to be feared; it is to be challenged.

People who only look for trophies
in life lead a shallow existence.

Mountain climbing and life are similar.
Both have peaks and valleys.

There is no pre-defined course to life;
you have to blaze your own trail.

To make the right turns in life, it's good
to have an idea where you are going.

*Life is like a poker game. Many people bluff
their way along but seldom win when they do.*

*A sure way to get bored with life
is to feel sorry for yourself.*

*Painting over the problems of life is a temporary
solution unless we first get rid of the rust.*

*If you think there are immediate solutions to
life's major problems, you are very nearsighted.*

*A barnyard and life have a lot in common.
You have to watch your step in both.*

*Life sometimes presents the wrong end
of the gift horse. In other words,
it is better to give than to receive.*

*Life is like a box; you have to pack it full
to get the most benefit out of it.*

> ## Life's journey can be a long and lonely highway when we feel sorry for ourselves.

How you approach the unknown—with
courage or with fear—determines
how far in life you go.

The only gravity you encounter on the
climb of life is that which you create.

Our lives and our world would be better if we
shared our Easter love every day of the year.

Don't blame others if you think your life
is in a rut. You built the road.

Remember that those you pass in the race of
life can catch up with you at a later date.

It is hard to navigate the curves in the road of life if you keep looking in the rear view mirror.

The Y's in the road make life interesting. You must make a decision which way to go or choose to remain at a standstill.

In the race of life, many people stumble over their egos and get left behind.

Life can be the pits if you keep digging holes.

The mountain of life has climbers and campers. Only the former have a chance to reach the top.

Create in life a legacy, not a resume.

The real challenges in life are the unhappy people we meet along the way.

194

*The losers in life don't know what they have
until they have thrown it away.*

*If you are satisfied with where you are in life,
be careful. You may get run over
by those who aren't.*

*A sure way to get lost in the maze of life
is to start cutting corners.*

*Life can be a fuzzy caterpillar or a beautiful
butterfly. It all depends on how we look at it.*

*To have a meaningful life, we have to
put more into it than we take out.*

*In our rush to get ahead in life, we have to
be careful not to leave others behind.*

*Don't try to clean up someone else's life until
you have shoveled out your own barnyard.*

*How far you go in life depends on
how you fill your tank of knowledge.*

*If you are going to fully play all four quarters
of the game of life, learn too play hurt.*

*Life is a puzzle, and people are the pieces.
The challenge is to create a picture of unity.*

*It is not which cards life deals you,
but how you play those cards that is important.*

*Life and love are only as exciting as
the effort you put into them.*

*If you understand that life is like a maze,
you won't give up when you reach
what appears to be a dead end.*

*If you want to tie a real knot in your life,
play both ends against the middle.*

*A sure way to complicate your own life
is to try to run the life of someone else.*

In life, choose to be a lifter, not a leaner.

One of the pitfalls in life is the unhappy people
who will try to drag you down with them.

*Life has a fast lane and a
slow lane and can become
a collision course when we
get the two confused.*

If you always let your heart be your guide, you
will never make a wrong turn on the road of life.

Life is tough, and a sure way
to let it defeat us is with self-pity.

Living is a given; life is about giving.

Life is like a balloon. The more you put into it,
the larger it gets; the more you take out,
the flatter it becomes.

Life and love need direction; just don't look back. You have already been there.

Life is a never-ending merry-go-round for those who travel in small circles.

Helping those below us rather than envying those above us is what life is all about.

If you want an empty carton of life, emphasize quantity over quality.

If you define change as a few loose coins, you will come up short in the big picture of life.

Many people can't spell procrastination, but that doesn't stop them from letting it impact their lives every day.

To get the most out of life, let your heart, not your head, be your guide.

*If you can't choose the high road over the low
road in life, you will always arrive at a dead end.*

*What you have done in the past
is not as important as what you will do
with the rest of your life.*

**Life can be like running water.
You can be the big drip of a leaky
faucet, or you can be the mighty
river that keeps moving along.**

*It is not where you are in life that counts.
It is what you did to get there and
where you are going from here.*

*Our worth is determined by what we
give back to life, not what we take out.*

*When you rest on your laurels, you
are at a standstill in the race of life.*

*Minor irritations in life can become major
eruptions if we let them get under our skin.*

*If you must compare your life to a barnyard,
think in terms of how green your grass will be.*

*The world would be a better place if
we learned to walk in the shoes of others.*

*Everyone's life begins and ends the same;
it is what we do in between that matters.*

*If it never rains on your parade, perhaps
you aren't marching to life's trumpet call.*

*When you ride through life on someone else's
fame, you will never toot your own horn.*

**The book of life will always
remain a mystery if we are afraid
to turn to the next page.**

*If "our" way was always better than "their" way,
life would need nothing but one-way streets.*

*Life can be a work of art,
but we have to be the artists.*

*A sure way to lose the race of life
is to be weighted down with a grudge.*

*Many people don't have room for others
in their lives because they take up
all the space for themselves.*

The only road map to life is the one you draw.

*Life has its ups and downs, and like a
roller coaster, you can face it with fear
or relax and enjoy the ride.*

To make life fun, learn how to laugh at yourself.

*If you buy into life's little pleasures,
you may end up with some big pains
you hadn't bargained for.*

**If you think life is like standing behind a
big elephant, quit following the elephant.**

*If you think your life resembles a bug
approaching a windshield, aim higher.*

*If you don't keep moving in life,
you will soon find yourself behind the times.*

*A sure way to have an empty life
is to lose interest in living.*

If you want a stagnant life, resist change.

*If you think you are leading a dog's life,
remember, it could be worse.
You could be a fireplug.*

*There are no seat belts on the roller coaster
of life; you need a tight grip and strong faith
to carry you along safely.*

*The best way to get nowhere fast on the
super highway of life is to follow the crowd.*

How fast you take the curves in the road of life
depends on how long you want to live.

If you think all of life is a ball, you are
living in an empty sphere.

Many of the problems we create in our lives
are a result of our inability to accept reality.

> ***Life owes us nothing. We are***
> ***born with a debt we can only***
> ***repay through good deeds.***

Many people don't discover the secrets of life
because they are afraid to open their doors.

It is how you handle the thorns that
can make your life a bed of roses.

A good way to get left behind in the
game of life is to play "what if."

*Many mistakes in life result from not knowing
the difference between perception and reality.*

*Life is like a garden. You have to nurture your
heart with love and weed your mind of hate.*

*Your life can take several directions,
but you are in control of the compass.*

*Life becomes tedious when the extreme
10 percent at either end take control of
the ordinary 80 percent in the middle.*

*Life can be an endless circle
if you don't look for new hills to climb.*

*Life may not be fair, but it is
better than the alternative.*

*The pattern of your life depends
on how well you tend to your knitting.*

*In life, blessings come and go. To keep
them flowing, we must learn to share.*

*Always remember that life is one big picture
made up of many small events.*

*The road of life is difficult to travel if you
have to push a big ego and haul a bad attitude.*

*If you feel life is passing you by, it is time
to buckle up, shift gears, and change lanes.*

*An optimist eagerly faces the unknown;
a pessimist can't even define reality.*

*If you think your life is in a rut,
you probably let routine
do the digging.*

*When perception becomes reality, you have
a foundation of sand upon which to build.*

*Life can be a bowl of cherries
if you learn how to spit out the seeds.*

*The biggest stumbling block in your life
may be the hard head between your ears.*

**Life can be exciting, but you
have to venture out of your
comfort zone to discover it.**

*It is hard to run the race of life if you're
carrying a big chip on your shoulder.*

*You are walking a dead end street in life
if you think your way is the only way.*

*If you think your life is the pits, remember, you
are the only one who can spit out the seeds.*

*A person who thinks that life is a lost cause
is afraid to give it a fighting chance.*

On the scale of life, let humility outweigh pride.

*Life has many ups and downs. Don't give in
to the lows or you won't have any highs.*

*It is hard to stay out of the ditches on the road
of life since we dig most of them ourselves.*

If you want a full life, load up on altruism.

**Life is full of problems. Finding
solutions is the key to personal
growth and world development.**

*When we focus on the big hurdles in life,
we often trip over the small stumbling blocks.*

Life is too short to have hate in our hearts.

*The path of life has many curves, and if
you don't keep your chin up, you won't
be able to see clearly where you are going.*

*Life's journey can be tedious if
you're hauling around guilt and anxiety.*

*If you are not willing to climb, you are going to
have a tough time on the bumpy road of life.*

*To have a tumultuous life,
always blame others for your mistakes.*

*If your life is in a rut, remember, you
created it by walking the same path every day.*

*Life is like a balloon. If you don't keep
filling it up, it will soon become empty.*

*Your cup of life will never runneth over
if you are afraid to fill it.*

*Every life has "worth." It's up to you to decide
if it will be worthless or worthwhile.*

*If you want to stumble through life, keep your
eyes closed to the pitfalls along the way.*

*When you cut corners on the road of life, you
have a good chance of ending up in a ditch.*

*When you realize there is no such thing
as a free ride in life, you get off
your high horse and get to work.*

**The world is a maze of
treasures, and the excitement of
life is to find as many as you can.**

*Life is a challenge to accept,
not a luxury to be handed to us.*

**Life can be a blast if you have
the nerve to light the fuse.**

The trip of life will be more enjoyable
if you unload your excess baggage.

The one constant in life is change, and if you
can't adapt, you will forever live in the past.

It is difficult at times to laugh at life,
but when you do, you truly begin to live.

Many bad breaks in life
are caused by indecision.

Never forget, we are all here by the luck of birth.

We all suffer from a fatal disease called life.
There is no cure, but a happy heart
is a soothing ointment.

Life is like the game of poker. You don't want to
throw in all your chips too early in the game.

Life is like a giant candy bar. Feel free
to take as many bites out of it as you can.

Many a happy life turns sour through self-pity.

*You miss the thrill of living when
you become a creature of habit.*

*Never forget that you set your own regulator
on the quality of your life.*

*How you deal with the rust in your life
depends on how hard you chip away at it
before you paint over it.*

*Trying to "keep up with the Joneses" is like
walking through life behind a well-fed mule.*

*When you overlook the little details in
the garden of life, you may be sowing
the seeds of a big mistake.*

*The quality of your life is like a bucket of water.
If you don't keep adding to it, it will evaporate.*

*Many of the detours we encounter
on the road of life are self-created.*

> ## *Life has many lessons to teach;
> unfortunately, many of us are
> slow learners.*

*If there are no skid marks on your road of life,
you probably haven't ventured very far.*

*The shortcuts you take on the road of life
sometimes end up being dead ends.*

If you want an empty life, think only of yourself.

*Life can be fun when you learn how to hold on
to good memories and let go of the bad.*

*If all you want out of life is what others have,
you will always be empty-handed.*

*If your aim in life is control of others,
you are missing the target.*

*In the race of life, anger and ego will
always make you stumble and fall.*

*Life is not always a downhill ride. We have to
pump hard to climb the next hill that appears.*

*If you think your world is like the center of
a life saver candy, expand your circle.*

*Personal development can be like growing a
grape. You can neglect it and let it die on the
vine or nurture it and turn it into fine wine.*

*The road of life is full of pot holes. You don't
have to fill them all; just try to avoid them.*

**The key to a happy life is
contribution, not retribution.**

*Life is a gift, and you have to unwrap it anew
each day to make it meaningful.*

*The best way to fall behind in life
is to rest on your laurels.*

A boring life is a creature of habit.

*If you are beginning to feel your life is too
predictable, take notice. You may be
on the road to nowhere.*

*There are many potholes on the road of life, but
a firm foundation is a great shock absorber.*

*When you stop using the word
"ending" and substitute "beginning,"
life takes on new meaning.*

*On the road of life, you may leave
people behind, but never forget
those who helped you get ahead.*

*You will never enjoy the riches of life
if you are stingy with love.*

*If you think your life is like standing under a tree
full of birds, don't look up. Move on.*

*The perfect person who criticizes others
all the time usually ends up playing solitaire
in the game of life.*

**Your compass of life will never
point in the right direction
if you are self-centered.**

*It is difficult to stay focused on your own course
in life if all you can see is what others have.*

*Just when you think you understand life,
you turn on the news and have to start
all over again trying to figure it out.*

Afterword

It is difficult for many people to face certain truths about themselves, and some of the *"thoughts"* in the preceding pages may give pause as one wonders *if the shoe fits.* If indeed we truthfully acknowledge it does, my advice is, *wear it; just remember not to lace it up too tight.* My hope is that some of the *thoughts* herein cause us all to stop and reflect on our own lives and the lives of those around us. Hopefully, the messages and humor contained within will make us better men and women with goals toward living in peace, toward not taking ourselves so seriously, and toward respect for our fellow man. If so, this book has served its purpose.

—HAYES MCCLERKIN